EMMANUEL JOSEPH

The Song of Us, How Music Reflects the Brain and the Evolution of Culture

Copyright © 2025 by Emmanuel Joseph

All rights reserved. No part of this publication may be reproduced, stored or transmitted in any form or by any means, electronic, mechanical, photocopying, recording, scanning, or otherwise without written permission from the publisher. It is illegal to copy this book, post it to a website, or distribute it by any other means without permission.

First edition

This book was professionally typeset on Reedsy.
Find out more at reedsy.com

Contents

1. Chapter 1: The Origins of Music — 1
2. Chapter 2: Music and the Brain — 3
3. Chapter 3: The Evolution of Musical Instruments — 4
4. Chapter 4: Music and Emotion — 6
5. Chapter 5: Music and Social Bonding — 8
6. Chapter 6: Music and Language — 10
7. Chapter 7: The Role of Music in Education — 12
8. Chapter 8: Music and Cultural Identity — 14
9. Chapter 9: Music and Technology — 15
10. Chapter 10: Music and Healing — 17
11. Chapter 11: Music and Creativity — 19
12. Chapter 12: The Future of Music — 21
13. Chapter 13: Music and Movement — 23
14. Chapter 14: Music and Innovation — 25
15. Chapter 15: The Future of Music and Society — 27

1

Chapter 1: The Origins of Music

Music is a universal aspect of human experience, deeply embedded in the fabric of our societies and cultures. It is an ancient form of expression, predating written language and historical records. Early humans used music to communicate, bond, and express emotions, long before they developed complex languages. The rhythm of drums, the melodies of flutes made from bones, and the harmonies created by early vocalizations all played a crucial role in the evolution of human culture.

The origins of music can be traced back to our ancestors, who likely imitated the sounds of nature. Birds singing, the rustling of leaves, and the rhythmic flow of water were all inspirations for early humans. These natural sounds were mimicked and incorporated into their own forms of expression, leading to the creation of the first musical instruments. Over time, music evolved from simple, primal sounds to more complex compositions, reflecting the growing sophistication of human societies.

As humans developed more advanced tools and techniques, they began to create a wider variety of musical instruments. The development of string instruments, such as the lyre and harp, and wind instruments, like the flute and trumpet, allowed for greater musical diversity. This expansion of musical possibilities helped to further enrich human culture and strengthen social bonds.

Music also played a crucial role in the development of religious and spiritual practices. Early humans used music in rituals and ceremonies to communicate with the divine, seek guidance, and express gratitude. These early musical traditions laid the foundation for the rich tapestry of musical expression that we see in the world today.

2

Chapter 2: Music and the Brain

The relationship between music and the brain is a complex and fascinating one. When we listen to music, our brains undergo a series of intricate processes that involve multiple regions and neural pathways. These processes help us to perceive, interpret, and respond to musical stimuli, creating a deeply emotional and immersive experience.

One of the key areas of the brain involved in music processing is the auditory cortex. This region is responsible for interpreting the various elements of sound, such as pitch, rhythm, and timbre. When we listen to music, the auditory cortex works in conjunction with other brain regions, such as the prefrontal cortex and the hippocampus, to create a coherent and meaningful musical experience.

The emotional impact of music is largely due to its ability to stimulate the brain's reward system. When we hear a piece of music that we enjoy, our brains release dopamine, a neurotransmitter associated with pleasure and reward. This release of dopamine creates a sense of euphoria and reinforces our desire to seek out and engage with music.

Music also has a unique ability to evoke memories and emotions. The hippocampus, a region of the brain involved in memory formation and retrieval, plays a crucial role in this process. When we hear a familiar song, the hippocampus helps to retrieve associated memories and emotions, creating a powerful sense of nostalgia and emotional connection.

3

Chapter 3: The Evolution of Musical Instruments

The development of musical instruments has been a crucial aspect of human cultural evolution. As societies grew more complex, so too did their musical traditions and the instruments they used. The evolution of musical instruments reflects the technological advancements and cultural exchanges that have shaped human history.

Early musical instruments were often made from natural materials, such as bones, shells, and stones. These primitive instruments were used to create simple rhythms and melodies, serving as a means of communication and expression. As humans developed more advanced tools and techniques, they began to create a wider variety of instruments with greater complexity and sophistication.

The development of string instruments, such as the lyre, harp, and violin, marked a significant milestone in the evolution of music. These instruments allowed for greater musical diversity and expression, enabling musicians to create intricate melodies and harmonies. The invention of the piano in the 18th century further revolutionized music, providing a versatile and dynamic instrument that could be used in a wide range of musical genres.

Wind instruments, such as the flute, clarinet, and trumpet, also played a crucial role in the evolution of music. These instruments allowed for

CHAPTER 3: THE EVOLUTION OF MUSICAL INSTRUMENTS

the creation of distinct and versatile sounds, contributing to the richness and diversity of musical expression. The development of brass instruments, such as the trombone and tuba, further expanded the possibilities of musical performance.

Percussion instruments, including drums, cymbals, and xylophones, have been used in musical traditions around the world for thousands of years. These instruments provide the rhythmic foundation for musical compositions, driving the tempo and adding depth to the overall sound. The evolution of percussion instruments reflects the diverse cultural influences and innovations that have shaped human history.

4

Chapter 4: Music and Emotion

Music has a profound ability to evoke and amplify emotions, making it a powerful tool for emotional expression and regulation. The connection between music and emotion is rooted in the brain's complex neural processes, which help us to perceive, interpret, and respond to musical stimuli in deeply emotional ways.

When we listen to music, our brains undergo a series of intricate processes that involve multiple regions and neural pathways. These processes help us to perceive, interpret, and respond to musical stimuli, creating a deeply emotional and immersive experience. One of the key areas of the brain involved in music processing is the limbic system, which plays a crucial role in regulating emotions.

The emotional impact of music is largely due to its ability to stimulate the brain's reward system. When we hear a piece of music that we enjoy, our brains release dopamine, a neurotransmitter associated with pleasure and reward. This release of dopamine creates a sense of euphoria and reinforces our desire to seek out and engage with music.

Music can also evoke a wide range of emotions, from joy and excitement to sadness and nostalgia. This emotional resonance is often influenced by the listener's personal experiences and memories associated with a particular piece of music. The hippocampus, a region of the brain involved in memory formation and retrieval, plays a crucial role in this process. When we hear a familiar song, the hippocampus helps to retrieve associated memories and emotions, creating a powerful sense of nostalgia and emotional connection.

5

Chapter 5: Music and Social Bonding

Music has long been a powerful tool for social bonding, helping to strengthen connections and foster a sense of community. Throughout human history, music has played a central role in rituals, ceremonies, and social gatherings, bringing people together and creating shared experiences.

One of the key ways in which music fosters social bonding is through its ability to synchronize the actions and emotions of individuals. When people engage in musical activities, such as singing, dancing, or playing instruments together, their brains release oxytocin, a hormone associated with social bonding and trust. This release of oxytocin helps to create a sense of unity and cooperation, strengthening social connections.

Music also serves as a means of communication and expression, allowing individuals to convey their thoughts, emotions, and cultural values. In many cultures, music is used to tell stories, pass down traditions, and celebrate important events. These shared musical experiences help to create a sense of identity and belonging, fostering social cohesion and cultural continuity.

In modern society, music continues to play a crucial role in social bonding. Concerts, festivals, and other musical events provide opportunities for people to come together and share in the joy of live music. The rise of digital technology has also made it easier for people to connect with others through music, whether by sharing playlists, participating in online music communities, or collaborating on virtual musical projects.

6

Chapter 6: Music and Language

The relationship between music and language is a deeply intertwined and complex one, with both forms of expression sharing many common features and processes. Both music and language rely on rhythm, pitch, and timbre to convey meaning and emotion, and both engage similar neural pathways in the brain.

One of the key similarities between music and language is their reliance on rhythm. In both forms of expression, rhythm serves as a foundational element, helping to organize and structure the flow of sounds. The ability to perceive and produce rhythmic patterns is a crucial aspect of both musical and linguistic competence, and this skill is thought to be rooted in the brain's temporal processing mechanisms.

Pitch is another important element shared by music and language. In music, pitch is used to create melodies and harmonies, while in language, pitch variations, known as intonation, help to convey meaning and emotion. The brain's ability to perceive and interpret pitch is essential for both musical and linguistic communication, and research has shown that musical training can enhance pitch discrimination skills in language as well.

Timbre, or the quality of a sound, is also an important feature of both music and language. In music, timbre helps to distinguish different instruments and voices, while in language, it contributes to the recognition of individual speakers and the emotional tone of speech. The brain's ability to perceive and analyze timbre is essential for both musical and linguistic processing, and this skill is thought to be supported by similar neural mechanisms.

Chapter 7: The Role of Music in Education

Music education has long been recognized as an important aspect of human development, offering numerous cognitive, emotional, and social benefits. The study of music helps to develop a wide range of skills, from auditory perception and motor coordination to emotional expression and social interaction.

One of the key benefits of music education is its ability to enhance cognitive skills. Research has shown that musical training can improve memory, attention, and problem-solving abilities, as well as enhance language and mathematical skills. These cognitive benefits are thought to be due to the brain's plasticity, or its ability to adapt and reorganize in response to musical stimuli.

Music education also plays a crucial role in emotional development. Through the study and performance of music, individuals learn to express and regulate their emotions, develop empathy, and build self-esteem. Music provides a safe and supportive environment for emotional exploration, helping individuals to develop a deeper understanding of themselves and others.

Social benefits of music education are equally significant. Participating in musical activities, such as choir, band, or orchestra, helps individuals to develop teamwork, cooperation, and communication skills. Music education provides opportunities for social interaction and collaboration, fostering a sense of community and belonging. These social benefits extend beyond the classroom, helping individuals to build strong, supportive relationships throughout their lives.

Music education also encourages cultural awareness and appreciation. By studying different musical traditions and genres, individuals gain a deeper understanding of diverse cultures and perspectives. This cultural awareness helps to promote tolerance, empathy, and global citizenship, fostering a more inclusive and harmonious society.

Despite the numerous benefits of music education, it is often undervalued and underfunded in many educational systems. Advocating for the importance of music education and ensuring its inclusion in curricula is essential for nurturing well-rounded, emotionally intelligent, and culturally aware individuals.

8

Chapter 8: Music and Cultural Identity

Music plays a crucial role in shaping and expressing cultural identity. It serves as a powerful means of communication, allowing individuals and communities to convey their values, beliefs, and traditions. Throughout history, music has been used to preserve cultural heritage, promote social cohesion, and assert cultural identity.

One of the key ways in which music reflects cultural identity is through its use in rituals and ceremonies. In many cultures, music is an integral part of religious and spiritual practices, serving as a means of connecting with the divine and expressing collective beliefs. These musical traditions help to reinforce cultural values and create a sense of shared identity and belonging.

Music also serves as a means of storytelling, allowing individuals to pass down stories, legends, and historical events through generations. In oral traditions, songs and ballads are used to preserve cultural history and transmit knowledge. These musical narratives help to maintain a sense of continuity and cultural identity, fostering a deep connection to the past.

In modern society, music continues to play a crucial role in shaping cultural identity. Popular music genres, such as hip-hop, reggae, and rock, often reflect the social and political issues faced by specific communities. These musical forms provide a platform for individuals to express their unique experiences and perspectives, contributing to the richness and diversity of global culture.

9

Chapter 9: Music and Technology

The relationship between music and technology has always been dynamic and transformative. Technological advancements have continuously shaped the way music is created, distributed, and consumed, influencing both the artistic process and the cultural impact of music.

The invention of the phonograph in the late 19th century marked a significant milestone in the history of music. For the first time, music could be recorded and reproduced, allowing it to reach a wider audience. This technological breakthrough revolutionized the music industry, paving the way for the development of new recording and playback technologies.

The advent of digital technology in the late 20th century brought about another major transformation in the music industry. The development of digital audio formats, such as MP3, and the rise of the internet made it easier than ever to distribute and access music. This democratization of music distribution allowed independent artists to reach global audiences, challenging the traditional music industry structure.

In recent years, advances in artificial intelligence and machine learning have further revolutionized the music industry. AI algorithms can now analyze and generate music, creating new possibilities for composition and production. These technological advancements have expanded the creative potential of musicians and opened up new avenues for musical exploration.

While technology has undoubtedly transformed the music industry, it has also raised important questions about the impact of digitalization on musical culture. Issues such as copyright, ownership, and the commercialization of music continue to be subjects of debate, as society navigates the complex relationship between music and technology.

10

Chapter 10: Music and Healing

Music has long been recognized for its therapeutic potential, offering a powerful means of healing and emotional expression. The use of music in therapeutic contexts, known as music therapy, has been shown to have numerous physical, emotional, and psychological benefits.

One of the key ways in which music promotes healing is through its ability to reduce stress and anxiety. Listening to calming music can help to lower heart rate, blood pressure, and cortisol levels, creating a sense of relaxation and well-being. Music therapy is often used in clinical settings to help patients manage pain, anxiety, and depression.

Music also has a unique ability to evoke emotions and facilitate emotional expression. In therapeutic contexts, music can be used to help individuals process and express their feelings, providing a safe and supportive environment for emotional exploration. This emotional release can be particularly beneficial for individuals who have experienced trauma or have difficulty expressing their emotions through words.

In addition to its emotional benefits, music therapy has been shown to have cognitive and motor benefits. For individuals with neurological conditions, such as stroke or Parkinson's disease, music therapy can help to improve motor coordination and cognitive function. The rhythmic and melodic elements of music provide structured cues that can aid in movement and memory.

The healing power of music extends beyond formal therapy settings. Many people use music as a means of self-care and emotional regulation in their daily lives. Whether through listening, singing, or playing an instrument, engaging with music can provide a sense of comfort, connection, and resilience.

11

Chapter 11: Music and Creativity

Music is a powerful catalyst for creativity, inspiring individuals to think, feel, and express themselves in new and innovative ways. The creative process in music involves a unique blend of technical skill, emotional expression, and imaginative exploration, making it a deeply fulfilling and transformative experience.

One of the key ways in which music fosters creativity is through its ability to evoke emotions and stimulate the imagination. When we listen to music, our brains create mental imagery and emotional associations, providing a rich source of inspiration for creative expression. Musicians often draw on these emotional and imaginative experiences to create new compositions and performances.

The collaborative nature of music also promotes creativity. Many musical genres and traditions involve group performance and improvisation, encouraging individuals to experiment and innovate together. This collaborative process helps to generate new ideas and perspectives, fostering a dynamic and evolving musical culture.

Music also provides a unique means of exploring and expressing identity. Through the creation and performance of music, individuals can convey their personal experiences, beliefs, and aspirations. This process of self-expression helps to cultivate a sense of authenticity and individuality, empowering individuals to explore and embrace their unique creative potential.

The creative potential of music is not limited to professional musicians. Many people engage in music-making as a hobby or recreational activity, finding joy and fulfillment in the process of creating and sharing music. Whether through songwriting, improvisation, or simply experimenting with new sounds, music provides a boundless canvas for creative exploration.

12

Chapter 12: The Future of Music

As we look to the future, the role of music in human culture continues to evolve and expand. Technological advancements, cultural shifts, and global interconnectedness are all shaping the future of music, creating new possibilities and challenges for musicians and audiences alike.

One of the key trends shaping the future of music is the rise of digital technology. The continued development of digital audio formats, streaming platforms, and social media has revolutionized the way music is created, distributed, and consumed. These technological advancements have made music more accessible and democratized, allowing independent artists to reach global audiences and challenging traditional industry structures.

Another important trend is the increasing focus on diversity and inclusion in the music industry. Musicians and audiences are increasingly advocating for greater representation and equity, challenging systemic biases and promoting a more inclusive musical culture. This movement is helping to amplify diverse voices and perspectives, enriching the global musical landscape.

The integration of artificial intelligence and machine learning is also transforming the future of music. AI algorithms can analyze and generate music, creating new possibilities for composition, production, and performance. While these technologies offer exciting opportunities for innovation, they also raise important questions about creativity, authorship, and the role of human musicians.

As we navigate the future of music, it is essential to recognize and celebrate the enduring power of music to connect, heal, and inspire. Regardless of technological advancements or cultural shifts, music will always remain a fundamental aspect of human experience, reflecting the depth and diversity of our shared humanity.

13

Chapter 13: Music and Movement

The connection between music and movement is a deeply rooted aspect of human culture. From dance to physical exercise, music has the power to inspire and enhance movement, creating a dynamic interplay between sound and motion. This relationship is reflected in the brain's neural processes, which help to coordinate and synchronize movement in response to musical stimuli.

One of the key areas of the brain involved in music and movement is the motor cortex, which is responsible for planning, controlling, and executing voluntary movements. When we listen to music, the motor cortex is activated, helping to coordinate our movements with the rhythmic patterns and tempo of the music. This activation is particularly pronounced when we engage in activities such as dancing or playing a musical instrument.

The cerebellum, a region of the brain involved in balance and coordination, also plays a crucial role in the relationship between music and movement. The cerebellum helps to fine-tune our movements in response to musical cues, ensuring that we maintain rhythm and synchronization. This process is essential for activities such as dancing, where precise timing and coordination are required.

Music can also enhance physical performance and motivation. Listening to upbeat, energetic music during exercise can help to increase endurance, reduce perceived effort, and improve overall performance. The brain's release of dopamine in response to music creates a sense of pleasure and reward, motivating individuals to push themselves further and achieve their physical goals.

14

Chapter 14: Music and Innovation

Innovation in music has been a driving force in the evolution of human culture, pushing the boundaries of artistic expression and technological advancement. Throughout history, musicians and composers have experimented with new sounds, techniques, and technologies, creating groundbreaking works that have reshaped the musical landscape.

One of the key factors driving innovation in music is the desire to explore and expand the possibilities of sound. Musicians and composers have long experimented with unconventional instruments, tuning systems, and performance techniques, seeking to create new and unique sonic experiences. This spirit of experimentation has led to the development of new musical genres and styles, from jazz and rock to electronic and experimental music.

Technological advancements have also played a crucial role in music innovation. The invention of new instruments, such as the electric guitar and synthesizer, has revolutionized the way music is created and performed. The development of recording and production technologies has opened up new possibilities for sound manipulation and composition, allowing artists to create complex and immersive musical works.

Collaboration and cultural exchange have also been important drivers of innovation in music. The blending of different musical traditions and styles has given rise to new genres and movements, reflecting the diverse influences and perspectives of a globalized world. This cross-cultural exchange has enriched the musical landscape, fostering creativity and inspiring new forms of artistic expression.

15

Chapter 15: The Future of Music and Society

As we look to the future, the relationship between music and society continues to evolve and expand. Music remains a powerful force for social change, cultural expression, and personal transformation, shaping the way we connect with ourselves and others.

One of the key trends shaping the future of music and society is the increasing emphasis on diversity and inclusion. Musicians and audiences are advocating for greater representation and equity, challenging systemic biases and promoting a more inclusive musical culture. This movement is helping to amplify diverse voices and perspectives, fostering a richer and more dynamic musical landscape.

The rise of digital technology and social media has also transformed the way we engage with music and society. Online platforms and streaming services have made music more accessible and democratized, allowing independent artists to reach global audiences and challenge traditional industry structures. This digital revolution has created new opportunities for collaboration, innovation, and cultural exchange.

Music continues to play a crucial role in social and political movements, serving as a powerful means of communication and expression. Musicians are using their art to raise awareness, inspire action, and promote social justice, reflecting the pressing issues and challenges of our time. This fusion of music and activism is helping to shape a more conscious and connected society.

As we navigate the future, it is essential to recognize the enduring power of music to connect, heal, and inspire. Regardless of technological advancements or cultural shifts, music will always remain a fundamental aspect of human experience, reflecting the depth and diversity of our shared humanity.

The Song of Us: How Music Reflects the Brain and the Evolution of Culture

In "The Song of Us," journey into the captivating world of music and discover its profound impact on the human brain and culture. This enlightening book unravels the mysteries of how music has shaped our evolution, bonded societies, and touched the deepest recesses of our minds.

Explore the origins of music, tracing its roots back to the dawn of humanity, and witness the remarkable evolution of musical instruments. Dive into the intricate relationship between music and the brain, and understand how melodies and rhythms evoke powerful emotions, stimulate memory, and enhance cognitive abilities.

Through twelve insightful chapters, this book delves into the roles of music in education, social bonding, and cultural identity. It also examines the transformative power of music in healing and creativity, and the innovative possibilities brought about by technological advancements.

"The Song of Us" celebrates the enduring power of music to connect, heal, and inspire. Whether you're a music enthusiast, a curious mind, or someone seeking a deeper understanding of the human experience, this book offers a harmonious blend of science, history, and culture that will resonate with readers of all backgrounds.

Enjoy the symphony of knowledge and inspiration that "The Song of Us" brings, and discover how music continues to shape our world and reflect the essence of who we are.

www.ingramcontent.com/pod-product-compliance
Lightning Source LLC
LaVergne TN
LVHW010444070526
838199LV00066B/6185